BRI

BO

RICHARD BRASSEY

Orion
Children's Books

Which queen is often shown with knives on her chariot wheels for cutting the legs off Romans?

Who is often known by the wrong name because a monk had bad handwriting?

BOUDICA

Who burned the whole of London to the ground and killed everyone who lived there?

Which queen do some people say is buried under Platform 8 at King's Cross station?

We don't know anything for sure about Boudica's early life. She must have been born in Britain not long before the Romans arrived in 43 AD. She was probably the daughter of a tribal leader and she probably grew up in a round wooden house with a thatched roof.

We do know that she married Prasutagus, the King of the Iceni, a British tribe who lived in the area of present-day Norfolk. The Roman historian Tacitus tells us they had two daughters. Since then history has got muddled. Some people have said they had three.

KING PRASUTAGUS'S PALACE

What's that?

It's an amphora. The Romans use it for putting olive oil in.

What's olive oil?

How many daughters do we have, Boudica?

The remains of a large wooden fortress discovered at Thetford might have been Prasutagus's palace. Only a few Roman things have been dug up there. It seems the old-fashioned Iceni didn't much go for the cool new Roman stuff.

When the Romans arrived to settle south-east Britain, they conquered some tribes immediately. They made peace with others. Others still, mainly in the west, united under their mysterious priests, the Druids, and kept on fighting. The Romans set out to defeat them.

ANGLESEY

DRUIDS

PAULINUS

WALES

We don't know much about the Druids except that they worshipped in sacred groves and seem to have thrown a lot of stuff and even people down deep wells as gifts to their gods. By 60 AD Paulinus, the Roman governor, had cornered them in their headquarters on the Welsh island of Anglesey.

London, known as Londinium, had not existed before the Romans began developing it as a busy sea port, so they made their capital at Colchester. Colchester had been the capital of the Iceni's neighbours, the Trinovantes, and they were not very happy about this.

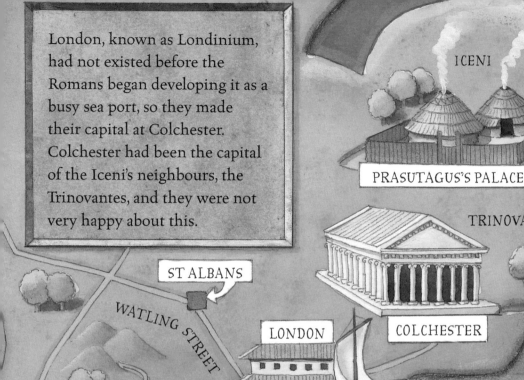

ICENI

PRASUTAGUS'S PALACE

TRINOVANTES

ST ALBANS

WATLING STREET

COLCHESTER

LONDON

TO FRANCE

A lot of the Trinovantes' land was seized and given to retired Roman soldiers. The Trinovantes were made to help build an enormous temple to the Emperor Claudius, who had just died and been made a god. All the conquered Britons were forced to pay heavy taxes.

Prasutagus had been allowed to remain as king of the Iceni so long as he did what the Romans said. When he suddenly died, his will left his kingdom to be divided equally between his daughters and the Emperor.

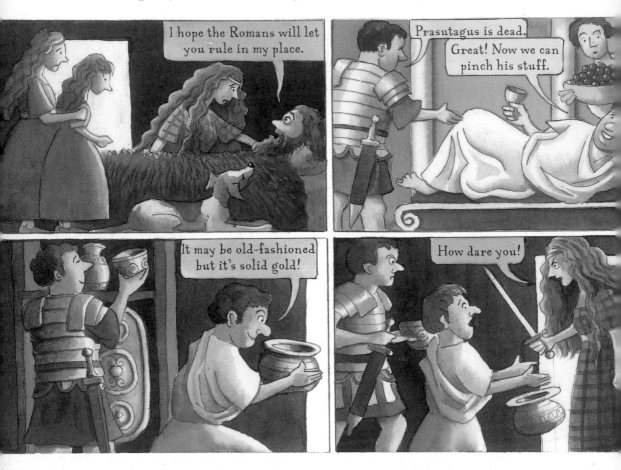

But the chief Roman tax collector, Catus, immediately sent in his men who began looting the Iceni's possessions. It's likely they even barged into the palace and began helping themselves to the royal treasure. Boudica was furious.

Boudica tried to stop them. The Romans dragged away her screaming daughters and then flogged the queen in front of her people. Because she had protested, they said that everything now belonged to the Emperor.

As soon as they released her, Boudica called a huge meeting of the Iceni and the Trinovantes. She demanded war on the Romans. Then, pulling a hare from under her cloak, she placed it on the ground to see which way it would run. A huge cheer went up as it raced off in the direction which meant good luck.

We have been robbed and cheated by the Romans. We have never united before but we must now or we will forget what freedom is.

It is said that 120,000 Iceni and Trinovantes marched on Colchester under Boudica's command. They couldn't have picked a better time. Paulinus and most of the Roman army were still far away in Anglesey.

Meanwhile, the Romans began noticing scary omens. Howling noises were heard. A vision of a ruined city was seen reflected in the Thames. The sea turned the colour of blood and shapes like dead bodies appeared on the shore.

In battle, the Britons used chariots which they drove wildly at their enemies while throwing spears. The Romans thought this was very old-fashioned but they admitted the Britons were skilled charioteers. They also often painted their bodies with blue dye called woad and fought with no clothes on.

There were no walls around Colchester because the Romans didn't think they needed any. Despite the omens, they were taken completely by surprise. They didn't even have time to send the women and children away.

When 2,000 men of the Ninth Legion, who were three days away, came marching down to help, Boudica's army ambushed and killed the lot . . . all except their commander, who fled back the way they came.

There was nobody to stop them sweeping into the town except the retired soldiers who fled in panic with the rest of the inhabitants to the only stone building, the half built temple of Claudius.

It became a trap. Boudica's men piled wood around the walls and set fire to it. Within two days every man, woman and child in the town had been killed, and the whole town burned to the ground.

Boudica's army was made up of farmers who were not used to discipline. They spent several days celebrating in Colchester before moving on to London.

This gave Paulinus time to race back to London from Anglesey with a small force. The whole town was in panic. All the wealthy people had fled. Although London was less than twenty years old, it had grown into a busy port and river crossing but it had no walls. It didn't even have any stone temples.

Let's get out of here!

Paulinus saw he couldn't defend it and advised everybody to leave. He raced back the way he'd come to meet his army who were on the road from Wales.

A few days later Boudica arrived. A layer of ash like the one at Colchester shows how she burned the whole place to the ground. Then she set off after Paulinus, destroying another town at St Albans on the way. The historian Dio says she killed 80,000 people in the three towns but he was probably exaggerating.

The two armies met somewhere halfway between Wales and London. Paulinus lined up his troops at the end of a narrow valley in front of a wood so nobody could attack him from behind.

Keep close order. When you have thrown your javelins, push forward with your shields and swords. Let the dead pile up.

Stop pushing at the back!

AARGH

There were about 12,000 Romans against at least 100,000 Britons. Boudica's soldiers were so sure they'd win, they'd brought their whole families along to watch from wagons, lined up in a semicircle at the mouth of the valley. Tacitus tells us that both leaders made long speeches of encouragement.

The Britons rushed into the valley but, because it was so narrow, only a few of them could attack the Romans at a time. The ones at the back got impatient and began pushing until the ones at the front were squashed against the Romans' shields and couldn't fight properly.

All day the Romans stabbed at them with their short swords, gradually pushing them back until they were trapped by their own wagons. It turned into a massacre. Tacitus says 80,000 of Boudica's men were killed and only 400 Romans . . . but he was probably exaggerating, as usual.

Those Britons who could fled the battlefield. Among them must have been Boudica. Tacitus says she gave up all for lost and poisoned herself and her daughters. Dio says she fell ill and died. We'll probably never know the truth.

Paulinus decided to teach the rebellious tribes a lesson. He sent soldiers all over the country to destroy their crops and seize their food stores. It caused a terrible famine. Thousands died.

LONDINIUM

Eventually a new governor replaced him, who felt this was no way to persuade the Britons it was cool to be part of the Roman Empire. His softer approach seems to have worked. The Romans stayed in Britain for the next 250 years. St Albans and Colchester were soon rebuilt. Many other towns grew up. London took off and within a few years it had replaced Colchester as the capital.

SOME BURNT FOOD AND BROKEN THINGS

pottery

figs

barley for beer

broad beans

waist-length, orangey-brown hair

clever for a woman

harsh voice

gold necklace

brooch

colourful tunic

thick cloak

very tall

DIO'S DESCRIPTION OF BOUDICA

Nearly all that we know about Boudica comes from the Roman historians, Tacitus and Dio. They didn't always get their facts right and usually tried to make the Romans look good so we can't believe everything they say.

But there's another way of finding out what happened. If you dig anywhere in Roman Colchester, London or St Albans, you'll find a thick layer of ash. Beneath it are things like coins and pottery which date from before 60 AD. Above it are later things. So Tacitus and Dio were right when they said Boudica burned all three towns to the ground.

dates

lentils

plums

amphorae

It's thought that a life-size bronze head of Claudius, found in a river nearby, may have been broken off a statue by Boudica's men and chucked in the water as a Druid-style offering.

> This must have been Boudica's mobile phone!

You have to be careful, though. Some people think almost anything they dig up from the right depth in the ground must have belonged to Boudica.

HEAD OF CLAUDIUS

LAYER OF ASH

HOW IS HER NAME SPELLED?

After the Romans left Britain Boudica was forgotten for a thousand years until a copy of Tacitus's history was found in a monastery in Italy. Tacitus spelled Boudica with two 'c's and the monk who made the copy looped the 'u' and the second 'c' so everybody thought she was Boadicea. In fact, Boudica meant victory so it's the same as modern-day Victoria.

DID SHE HAVE SCYTHES ON HER CHARIOT WHEELS?

If she did, they'd probably soon have caught on something and tipped her over. The idea seems to come from a bad translation in another part of Dio's history which made an eighteenth century artist think chariots often had blades on their wheels. It was such a scary idea that it stuck, but it's highly unlikely.

STONEHENGE
One of the first places to be suggested just because it's old. In fact it's so old it was built long before Boudica's time.

PECKHAM RYE, SOUTH LONDON
It's anybody's guess how the story arose that Boudica fought her last battle and is buried here. There's not a shred of evidence.

WHERE IS SHE BURIED?
Dio tells us that Boudica had a very expensive funeral. People soon started to wonder where she was buried and if there was any treasure there. Any number of places have been suggested but nobody really has a clue. She's probably buried near the final battlefield . . . wherever that was!

PLATFORM 8, KING'S CROSS STATION
Some people thought the final battle took place in North London and that she lies beneath what is now King's Cross Station . . . though why Platform 8 is a mystery!

PARLIAMENT HILL, HAMPSTEAD
There was a mound here which people used to call 'Boudica's grave'. Excavation in the nineteenth century showed it was nothing more than a rather new rubbish dump.

The Romans had been very shocked by Boudica. They didn't think politics or fighting wars was women's business. Some of them even thought the reason a woman had led an army against them was the gods' way of saying that the Emperor Nero was just too girly.

Boudica is ten times the man he is!

All he does is play his lyre . . .

. . . and put on make-up

She's so tall and comely, she's just like Boadicea.

Women didn't run things in England for another thousand years, so a lot of men strongly disapproved when Elizabeth I became queen in 1558. But after she turned out to be such a strong ruler and beat the Spanish Armada, she was often compared with Boudica. Boudica's story became a popular subject for plays.

Although the Victorians liked to compare their empire to the Roman Empire, they also compared their queen to Boudica. Queen Victoria's husband, Albert, took a lot of interest in a huge statue of Boudica, which sculptor Thomas Thorneycroft worked on for thirty years . . . and still hadn't quite finished when he died.

The suffragettes, who campaigned for women to be allowed to vote at the beginning of the twentieth century, also saw Boudica as an example of a woman who could run things just as well as any man.

Twenty years after Thorneycroft died, his statue of Boudica was finally erected next to Westminster Bridge and the House of Commons. As Winston Churchill, the famous Second World War prime minister, said: 'Her monument reminds us of the harsh cry of "Liberty or death" which has echoed down the ages.'

Boadicea – Boudicca, Queen of the Iceni who died in AD 61 after leading her people against the Roman invader.

It was a ferocious uprising.

Here she stands as though ready to fight off any invader who might foolishly try to cross the Thames as the Romans did 2,000 years ago.